The Power of

NLP

To you, I am so pleased you have picked this book up. I am going to share with you the power of neuro linguistic programming and how simple but fascinating this stuff is. I will share with you the power this has had in my life and how I overcame so much, it may not be an easy read and there may be some triggers within the pages (full disclaimer) but I think it is important to share with you why I am so passionate about sharing the power of NLP with you and an example of how it can impact someone's life so much. I hope you enjoy NLP as much as I do. Enjoy! Rebecca x

About the author:

Rebecca is a best selling author, mum to 2 girls and she teaches entrepreneurial women the art and science of how the mind works. You'll find her delivering content on neuro-linguistic programming, Breakthrough Coaching, Time Line Therapy, Positive Psychology, EFT and Energy. She is regularly seen in Stylist Magazine, Cosmopolitan, Marie Claire, Glamour, BBC, Harper's Bazaar and more. Rebecca has built a successful coaching and training business and teaches other individuals certifications in coaching and NLP and how to release limitations and become their own version of success.

Welcome to the book:

Welcome to my world of neuro linguistic programming. I absolutely love this stuff and I am really excited for you to dive in and learn all about the power of the mind and how the mind works.

This stuff has completely changed my life as you will learn within the first chapter. I kinda feel like I need to apologise in advance as I was going through such a dark time when I first found neuro linguistic programming and I couldn't think of a better way to share with you how my life was actually happening without sharing some of my journal entries at that time.

It may be a hard read and there may be some triggers within the pages, just know that I overcame this and now although reading it back still twinges some of my emotional heart strings remembering that time, I am fully healed thanks to the power of NLP and other work that I teach within my courses.

Trigger warnings are around mental health, post natal depression, anxiety, depression, obsessive compulsive disorder, self harm and suicidal thoughts. Wow, seeing them there in front of me like that makes me think that there is a lot, and there is. I have experienced all of these things and because of that I am talking about them in this book as that is how I have written it.

It's still scary to share the depths of my soul, but I hope it helps to illustrate the difference between the version of me then and the version of me now after learning NLP and applying it into my life.

I have only been able to move through these challenges because of what I have learnt and what I am teaching you within these pages.

Please bear in mind that within NLP there is so.much.jargon. I have written this book in the best way I know how, as if we are having a conversation. That was my aim anyway, however there are parts where I have to add in the jargon and then I have broken down what it all means to demystify it all. I really do think sometimes that the long words that are used are unnecessary, but hey, it was the 70's and it was created by men.

My intention with this book is to share with you the power of NLP as I share parts of my journey weaved into the book, in the hope that you will understand parts of NLP that you can apply and use in a reflective way in your own life. Perhaps as you are going through the book you may decide you want to take your NLP knowledge further and you want to take the next steps to train in NLP with me and my company The Yes I Can Method.

As you are going through the book please do share with me your journey, your insights and self discoveries. You can find me here:

Instagram - @Rebecca.Lockwood
Facebook - Rebecca Lockwood
Website - www.RebeccaLockwood.org.Uk

The training business pages:

Instagram - @the_yes_i_can_method_academy
Facebook - The Yes I Can Method Academy
Website - www.YesICanMethod.com

There are also lots and lots of extra resources, free training and our paid certification programs and training over on the training website www.YesICanMethod.com so make sure you check them out before you start too!

Welcome to the power of NLP.

Grab a cuppa, sit down and let's dive in.

Contents

Introduction

I was so excited when I was planning the arrival of my first child. When my baby arrived, things became confusing and I found myself feeling lost and I didn't understand why I felt so bad. I felt so bad and then I felt guilty for feeling that way, which made me feel even worse and I ended up in this spiral of negative loop feeling worse and worse and then judging myself for feeling so bad.

I began to feel hopeless and would cry uncontrollably. I was suffering from postnatal depression (PND), I didn't even recognise the problem was because of me, I just wanted it all to go away, I just felt so low and helpless.

Before having my baby I had been diagnosed with OCD - obsessive compulsive disorder and I was struggling with obsessive thoughts. Thankfully for me it wasn't any behaviour, but that didn't make it any easier. The thoughts were so dark and scary and I was disguised with myself all the time.

At first I couldn't share it with anyone because I didn't want to acknowledge it myself. I couldn't bring myself to admit I had a problem let alone speak to anyone else about it.

The doctor told me I had Obsessive Compulsive Disorder (OCD) – repetitive thoughts you don't want to think. In my case, the thoughts were about self-harm and taking my life, although I have never actually self-harmed or understood why the thoughts were there. At the time, she told me that OCD stays with you for life. That was in 2015, and the thoughts did release and became less consistent when I stumbled across Neuro Linguistic Programming (NLP) and hypnotherapy.

As a society we need to open up more about these situations and that is why I find the courage to openly share my experiences with you. Having overcome this experience through learning neuro-linguistic programming and applying it to myself I feel driven to teach others the power of understanding your mind and to allow yourself to be more human.

_____

Blog Entry Oct 2015: 'Since having my baby I've really struggled with my thoughts. I struggled with them before anyway, but even more so after my beautiful baby. I don't understand why I would think the way I do. I am so anxious and tense. I will feel like I am on top of the world, she is amazing, I couldn't have asked for anything more. Everything will be going swimmingly, I will be organised, I will be doing work. I will have lots to do and my baby is superb. And BAM! – it will creep into my mind like a burglar in the night. This is hard to say and to have to read, but a lot of this blog will be. I think about hurting myself. On a daily basis. It will smack me in the face whilst I'm singing along to my favourite songs. It will peer into my unwanted memories when I'm least expecting it. It's like a monster, a monster that comes out of the dark and leaves me gasping for air… And what's going on here isn't even the worst of my memories, of my feelings and thoughts.'

Blog Entry Oct 2015: 'I feel as though I am being dramatic and attention-seeking so I don't want to tell anyone but I just can't help it. I don't know what to do to make it go away. To make myself feel better. I just want to not be here anymore. I feel as though I am being selfish. But I just can't help it.'

My family came round after we got home from the hospital and they all commented on how clean the house was, and how amazing I was doing to be on top of everything. What they didn't know was how I was really feeling inside. I didn't even really understand how I was feeling inside. The only thing I knew was that I couldn't stop crying, I had no idea what was going on half the time due to the medication from the surgery, and I was exhausted. The medication also gave me night terrors. I remember, once, waking up above my daughter's moses basket, which was next to our bed, and being terrified. I couldn't move. This happened several times in the first few weeks. I would wake up but not be able to move – feeling as though I was scratching at my eyes to be able to see but not being able to do anything, move or speak. I knew then that I had to get off the medication I was on ASAP and, even though I went to the doctor and was given new medication for the pain, I still didn't open up about my feelings of hopelessness and confusion.

It's so important to know how to recognise this in yourself and to seek support and help. Even if it's just talking to someone, picking up the phone and just saying out loud how you feel.

Remember that the feelings are temporary, and they will pass. After almost a full year in silence, I finally accepted help from the doctors, was prescribed antidepressants and referred for counselling and psychotherapy.

I can't remember what finally made me accept the help, I just came to a time where I knew it was what I needed. I made an appointment with my doctor and I just blurted out how bad I was feeling.

Blog Entry March 2016: 'My doctor has increased my antidepressant medication and referred me for counselling. The counselling department called and said they need to assess whether I need a counsellor or a psychologist. I'm not sure what the difference is to be honest. I don't really want to see either, I just want to forget about my thoughts and go to sleep. I've been working hard on my mindset to keep myself on track but it is so hard. I listen to a lot of Les Brown and Tony Robbins, I read a lot of self-help mindset growth books and I tell myself every day is going to be a good day. It just feels like it's hitting deaf ears at the moment and I just feel like I can't be bothered. I feel tired of life and my thoughts.'

It's crazy to think about it now but it was through the suffering in silence and attempting to help myself with personal development that I was able to discover the path I am on now. I had been listening to Tony Robbins Unlimited Power on repeat almost every day for that full year when one day I heard him say, 'NLP – Neuro Linguistic Programming'. At that moment I knew I needed to go and study NLP. I had been listening to the CD on repeat for a full year and had never heard him say NLP before.

Learning all about how I could change the way I was thinking, change the representation of anything I wanted to in my mind fascinated me. I worked on my mindset, limiting beliefs and anxiety and began to see a huge transformation in my life and in the way I was feeling.

It was all inside, everything I ever needed was just inside of me the whole time, I just never knew it. After studying NLP, I felt an almost instant shift. My post natal depression, my negative experiences of the past, washed over me and I created a whole new meaning to my life. My future became brighter and full of possibility. I didn't realise at the time, but I was so negative towards myself and I really was unkind and judgemental about who I was and how I was living my life. I learned to release all judgements towards myself and to no longer feel the need to control anything outside of myself. Instead I ask myself 'What CAN I control here?' And focused on myself internally.

_____

Blog Entry Dec 2016: 'When you doubt, when you're unsure of which way to turn,
listen, listen to yourself. Deep inside. You know what to do.
I've realised, I don't need any more money than I'm getting from the day job. I have loads of time too, I want to interview inspiring people, get sponsors from businesses that make a difference and donate the money to a good

cause. Helping young girls when leaving school. Helping young girls at school with vulnerability. Helping parents with depression, anxiety, baby blues. I just don't want anyone to have to go through what I've gone through. No one needs this haunting them for life. Whether it's helping them forgive and forget, or not steer in the wrong direction in the first place. I want to make a difference. You know what, I've had a pretty difficult life. But that's ok.

_____

Ask yourself: What defines you?

You are the one who decides who you are. When you hear that voice inside your head that says:

"You never finished your dancing exams."
"You never finished college."
"You didn't go to university.'"
"You got kicked out of school before your exams and failed miserably."
"You're not capable of this, who the hell do you think you are?"
"You have no qualifications."

Just remember, that was then and this is now. We all feel vulnerable, remember when you're feeling this way, you're not the only one.

I now live life by the mantra: 'Change your mind, Change your life'

I have studied Neuro-Linguistic Programming to the highest level and now I run my own NLP training business, supporting other individuals to live a more empowered life and become the best possible version of themselves regardless of their past, traumas or experiences.

In the darkest times, in the moments that feel like the worse times of your life, NLP can help you allow them to empower you, to give negative experiences new meaning and allow you to learn from them as much as you can in a way that is positive.

The idea after learning NLP is that you should be able to empower yourself by knowing you are in control of your life, your actions and your emotions so you can just show up as the best possible version of you, but also be ok with not being too. As I learned, you can change your mind, which will change your life.

Within this book I am going to introduce to you the concept of Neuro-Linguistic Programming.

I am going to teach you in the best way I can how to utilise the tools and techniques within NLP by giving you examples from my own life, I think that is important because you will see from the inside out how this stuff will impact you and if you do decide to study NLP fully, also how it will impact your clients. Throughout the book I will tell you my own personal stories, stories from my clients and students so you can also see and understand different perspectives and examples on how this stuff all fits together. I will show you the content that supported me to turn my life around and change my mind, which led my life to change.

We are powerful beings, and the world works for us in mysterious ways. Within this book I am going to use science based information, facts based on research done over the years through the work on Neuro-Linguistic Programming.

I have not created this method of work, I am a student just as you are. I have learnt as much as I can about NLP, the mind, the science behind how it all works and now I bring it to you and my students within my courses. You can also find out more about the courses I deliver in NLP at rebeccalockwood.org.uk

I invite you to learn with me and I welcome you on this journey, I am here each step of the way.

Let's get started.

When doing any transformational work or learning something new it's always important to get it down on paper and become clear on what goals and outcomes you aim to achieve through going through the content.

It always helps to be intentional about what you are doing and why so you get the very most out of it. When you know what you want as an outcome you can then ensure you are meeting your needs.

Outcomes & Goals

Write on a piece of paper what you want to achieve from reading this book.

Write it as if you have already achieved it.

When you write it as if you have already achieved it, you are activating the part of your brain that will notice all of the opportunities to make it happen much faster, and we will learn all about this soon. It creates a pull within the subconscious and makes the part of your brain called the reticular activating system notice the things in your reality that can help you make this happen.

Questions to answer:

What do you want to get out of this book?

What are you reading for?

How will you feel once you have completed the book?

To achieve the very best from this book I suggest you read through it and allow yourself to soak up the knowledge and learning. Don't be concerned about the big picture, just allow yourself to take it all in as it comes. Once you have read the book I suggest you then go back through it and re read it. Make notes, put some sticky notes into the sections that you want to re read and refer back to, and if at points you find yourself wanting to take some actions write them down straight away and act upon them as you feel compelled to do so.

Chapter 1: Definition of NLP

When I first learnt about how our minds work and why they work this way I was so blown away just by having an understanding of the mind and the way we think. Why we behave the way we do and what we do. So much stuff we do stems back to our past and the distorted stories we tell ourselves about who we are and our place in the world.

Having this understanding made so much sense to me and I realised that one of the reasons why I was so poorly with depression was because of the way I was distorting information.

Something that happened when we were young, within our imprint period between the ages of 0-7 can linger around for the rest of our lives if we are not aware of it. I have had students telling me that they are in their 50's and they have only just now released these limiting stories they were telling themselves from when they were 7!

So many of us walk around in life with these stories like a backpack, and it projects out into the world like a projector, we then act in accordance with this and these are the eyes we are seeing the world through. Often we are not aware of this and have no idea it is happening.

Definition of NLP

Neuro: The nervous system (the mind), through which our experience is processed via our five senses:

- Visual
- Auditory
- Kinaesthetic
- Olfactory
- Gustatory

Neuro is the nervous system, understanding the mind and how we think.

Linguistic: Language and other nonverbal communication systems through which our neural representations are coded, ordered and given meaning.

Includes:

- Pictures
- Sounds
- Feelings
- Tastes
- Smells
- Words (self talk)

Linguistic is the language of the mind and understanding the way we communicate to ourselves and the world around us.

Programming: The ability to discover and utilise the programs that we run (our communication to ourselves and others) in our neurological systems to achieve our specific and desired outcomes.

Programming is the way we behave and understanding the way your mind is programmed to behave currently and how to make changes if you'd like to.

In other words, NLP is how we use the language of the mind to consistently achieve our specific and desired outcomes.

I like to say, Neuro Linguistic programming is the art and science of being the best possible version of yourself.

NLP is all about how you think, and how you can think more effectively. When you understand your mind and the way you are filtering in information you can then understand if you are distorting information too. NLP really helps you to clear out your mind if you need to.

I like to think of NLP like a clear up. If we think of life like a garden path. We have this path that we are walking down and along the way there are leaves scattered on the floor, there are trees that may have fallen down and other things that may block our path forward. NLP is what helps you clear these things out of the way so that it is much easier to make your way down your path. You may come to a point where there is a gate or a locked door. NLP is the key to unlocking these barriers and challenges so that you can continue on your path of life. It's giving you a good clear up of everything you no longer need, it supports you to utilise the behaviours and habits in your life that will support you and release the behaviours and habits that you no longer need. It helps you to be more effective and it really makes life feel much easier and lighter.

NLP supports you to change yourself very quickly and become the best and most efficient possible version of yourself. Learning NLP is a process that continues throughout life and never ends because once you learn it you become so aware of communication with others and with the world around you, it seriously opens your eyes. You become aware of how others are thinking and communicating, how you are thinking and communicating and it allows you to see things from different perspectives.

As you read through this book and learn the power of NLP you will see it really is like common sense on steroids. It helps you understand how your mind works, why you think the way that you think and how you communicate to yourself and to others.

NLP was developed in the early 1970s by an associate professor of linguistics, John Grinder and a psychology student, Richard Bandler who was at the University of California at Santa Cruz. They had observed that people with similar education, training, background, and years of experience were achieving widely varying results ranging from wonderful to mediocre.

They wanted to know the secrets of effective people. What makes them perform and accomplish things? They were especially interested in the possibility of being able to duplicate what the really successful people were doing so that then others could follow these same steps and also get amazing results too, they called this modelling.

A lot of the work in NLP was created by modelling. Modelling the famous hypnotherapist Milton Erickson and the famous family therapist Virginia Satir. Many of the techniques I teach within my NLP practitioner course are based on the success these therapists achieved with their patients.

Richard and John decided to model human excellence. They looked at factors such as education, business and therapy. They then focused on the communication aspect. They started studying how successful people communicated (verbal language, body language, eye movements). It was during this period of modelling the behavioural activity of Virginia Satir, the founder of Family Therapy, Fritz Perls, the founder of Gestalt Therapy and Milton H Erickson, a renowned Hypnotherapist that NLP was truly born.

By modelling their behaviour, John Grinder and Richard Bandler were able to make out patterns of thinking that assisted in the subject's success. The two came to the conclusion that the brain can learn the healthy patterns and behaviours and that this would bring about positive physical and emotional effects. What emerged from their work came to be known as Neuro Linguistic Programming.

The basic thinking of NLP is that the words we use reflect an inner, unconscious perception of our problems. If these words and perceptions are inaccurate, they will create an underlying problem as long as we continue to use and to think about them. Our attitudes are, in a sense, a self-fulfilling prophecy. The way we feel will project out in our behaviours which gives us our results in life, and if these are not supporting us to be effective then we can learn to change them too by using the power of NLP.

What we believe and how we perceive ourselves and the world around us determines how we project ourselves out into the world. Perception is projection. We then act in accordance with that, which creates our behaviours, our outcomes and our results. What we believe inside our minds really determines our whole life and the building blocks of our reality.

NLP is a therapy that utilises the analysis of words, phrases and non-verbal language such as facial expressions, eye movements, and body movements to gain insights into the physical and emotional state of an individual.

After identifying issues and distortions with the individual's perception and inner unconscious processing patterns, an experienced NLP coach will be able to help someone to understand the root cause of their problems. The therapist will then help the individual to remodel their thoughts and mental associations in order to help them understand why they were thinking that way and how to make the changes desired. These preconceived associations may be keeping the individual from achieving the success and results they deserve.

It's important to understand what makes us human and why we feel and think the way that we do. NLP really helps to demystify this and creates an understanding of the mind, the way you feel and the way you think to support you whenever you may feel negative, lonely, down, anxious, worried or any other feelings that you may be confused about.

NLP helps people to change any unhealthy traits and replaces them with the outcomes that you want instead. It works with the brain and changes neural networks to create different behaviours and thought patterns.

Chapter 2: So what is the model of communication?

Here you will see a diagram that I am going to refer to called the model of communication. This is part of the NLP work and explains how we think and filter information in through our brain and then how we project this information out into the world which creates our version of reality.

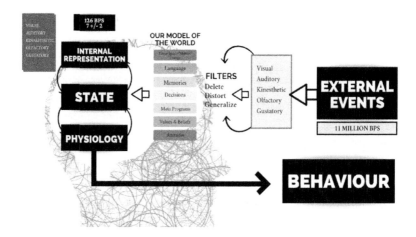

External Events: These are events that happen in our lives. Things that happen all around us at all times. It doesn't have to be anything magical like a party, it literally is all the stuff you can see around you now when you look around wherever you are.

It is estimated that we have around 11 million bits of information per second (BPS) potentially in our awareness. Now, remember this was created in the 70's, so I would suggest that it may be a lot more than that now due to the advancement of technology and our smartphones and devices.

These come in through our senses, what we can see (visual) , what we can hear (auditory) , what we can feel (kinaesthetic) , what we can smell (olfactory) and what we can taste (gustatory).

Delete, Distort, Generalise: We then delete, distort and generalise this information. Think about it like this. We have something called a Reticular Activating System, also known as a RAS. This is the part of our brain that decides which pieces of information we are going to pay attention to because we couldn't possibly pay attention to it all at the same time we would be in constant overload. I will talk to you more about the RAS soon. We filter the information that comes in based on what our brain knows (or thinks) it needs to notice.

We choose how to pay attention to information by our goals, our intentions, what we have going on in life at the moment, what we are currently paying attention to and even what we are currently watching on tv or listening to has an impact on how we delete, distort and generalise information.

Imagine you have millions of straws dropping down on you and you grasp as many as you can, out of that 2 million you may grasp around 130, which is the amount of information we can take in at any time. We delete, distort and generalise based on the time, space, matter, energy, language, memories, decisions, our personality types (meta programs), our values, beliefs, our attitudes and our goals in life.

We have to delete information because we couldn't possibly take in millions of bits of information at one time or we would go into overload. Have you ever had too many things playing at a time and felt overwhelmed!? It would be like that x a million!

Our brains have to filter this information down for us to be able to make sense of it and do something with it.

We also distort information based on our beliefs, for example you may think that someone who is looking over at you has a certain thought or belief about you. Chances are, they are not thinking about you at all, but because you are distorting the information you are creating a whole meaning to this event that may not be true to someone else.

Everything we think, everything we believe, everything we filter into our minds is just a distorted version of the truth in that moment in time based on our systems. It is not necessarily the truth, it is just our version of the truth in that moment in time. It is our truth, but it is also distorted based on so many things that we do have control over and I will speak about this throughout the book.

Perception is projection, what you are thinking about in your mind projects out into the world and is what you will see. You do not believe what you see, you see what you believe. So let's say you have a limiting belief about not being able to do something, you may think that someone else doesn't believe in you. It really doesn't have anything to do with the other person, it really is all about you and how you perceive yourself and that is how you are filtering certain information through.

A while ago I remember I had hit a big goal. It was to reach a big sales target in my business. It had been so hard and took me years to do it. When I finally did achieve it I said to my husband "See, I told you I could do it. You doubted me so much, and look, now I have done it" he replied saying he had never once doubted me and he had never said that. He said he had always and does always believe in me. The truth was that I had doubted myself, that was a bit realisation for me. I hadn't even realised I had doubted myself, a good indication that you have limiting beliefs is you thinking other people think certain things about you that you may actually just believe about yourself. We will talk more about this later.

We grasp around 130 pieces of information from the 2 million and then this is distorted and generalised, that gets stored as a memory. Before it gets stored we create an image in our mind of the event. That image gives us a feeling and determines how we feel about that event.

We then come to our model of the world.

Our model of the world is made up from the following and determines who we think we are as people, how we think about our place in the world and how we act based on that. Things that we believe can be thought of as facts, but really these are just our internal thoughts and perceptions and we all think differently. Everything we think is just a distorted perception of that moment in time based on our model of the world.

Even if you have siblings that had the same upbringing as you, your model of the world will be very different because of all of these things together.

We all have a different model of the world and we all experience life differently. Our model of the world is the reason we all have different beliefs, we enjoy different things and have different personalities.

Let's have a look at each of these individually.

Time/Space/Matter/Energy: We are impacted by the way we perceive time, but also the way we move and the energy we have around us. This can be internally and externally. Internally we feel, we have emotions, we think, we move, this is all energy.

Everything around us is also energy and how we perceive this is very important in our lives. I won't go deep into quantum physics within this book as that is a different chat all together, but I do want to introduce this here because everything we do is energy and everything we see is energy. The universe is literally made up of energy and so are we. We are made out of the same stuff. It is all energy. How we perceive this and what we do with this information has a huge impact on our lives.

Language: The language we use and the words we use to describe everything are so important. When we use certain words we create meanings and internal representations of them. Everyone will create a different internal representation of different words.

Have you ever been having a conversation with someone and completely misunderstood what they meant?

This is because you created a different meaning to the words that were used than they did.

Recently we had to call the garage to come out and fix the car and the mechanic said "I will try to get up to you in the morning" for me, I was like, well are you going to try or are you actually going to come as if not then I will call someone else as my car needs fixing!"

He meant he was coming, however, due to the language that was used I wasn't sure if that's what he meant. It's not that I was trying to be funny or rude, I just needed to know if he was coming or not. It's so easy to be misunderstood and misunderstand others when it comes to language.

Simple language can create varying meanings so be aware that it can be easy to misunderstand people and to be misunderstood by people too.

The language that we use makes up part of our model of the world.

Memories: Our memories and past experiences make up the personality we have today. We can see a completely new chair for example, but we know it is a chair because we know what a chair is.

Our memories that we have of ourselves, our childhoods, our loved ones. The things we experience and how we remember them has a huge impact on how we see the world and how we see ourselves.

We also process our memories in different ways. Sometimes our memories can be unconscious, sometimes they can be metaphoric, meaning that they have a certain meaning to them. They can also be constructed, so for example if a parent has told you a story about something that happened in your childhood and you only created a memory based on the information that was given to you through these stories then they are constructed.

Also remember, that our memories can also be just a distorted version of the truth in that moment in time based on our model of the world in that age. We then carry this through our lives and project it out into the world.

Our distorted version of our memories can also be the basis of our beliefs and impact our lives forever. I have had experiences where memories that I distorted from the age of 5 or 6 have impacted my life up until I changed the distortion of them when I first trained in NLP at 24 years old. Crazy stuff!

I want to give you an example of this as I think you need to understand this a bit more.

When I was young I danced at a local dance school (I still dance now, it is the one constant I have had in my life). I loved it and I was in my element on the dance floor. I was offered a solo part in the show and was over the moon. Although the solo part never came. It was mentioned to me numerous times but then nothing happened and I didn't get the solo part. I was confused and it made me believe that I wasn't good enough to actually do it. This impacted my life so much and I projected this out into the world as a belief of "I am not good enough or worthy enough to have anything".

I mean thinking about this now it feels crazy that this thing impacted my life so much. It wasn't a traumatic experience or anything like that, and that is also important to remember. Memories and experiences do not have to be traumatic to have an impact in your life.

It's also important to mention that I didn't consciously know that this memory and how I had distorted it was having an impact on my life, I was just acting in accordance with it based on my model of the world.

When I first trained in NLP and realized this was one of the things that I had been distorting and then projecting out into the world I realized that it has had a huge impact in so many other aspects of my life too including but not limited to…

- Closing a successful fashion business down after 3 years of growth
- Not feeling I was worthy of being spoken about highly in the media
- Having negative thoughts
- Negative self talk and beating myself up about anything that I do well, and anything I didn't do well
- Spoiling my relationships
- Causing arguments in relationships

There were so many areas of my life that it impacted. I also realized that my distortion wasn't correct either. My mum struggled with paying for my dancing lessons to go to the dance school in the first place, let alone to pay for private lessons to get a solo part. It wasn't anything to do with me.

Decisions: The decisions that we have made in the past. Decisions may create new beliefs, or may just affect our perceptions through time. The problem with many decisions is that they were made either unconsciously or at a very early age, and are forgotten by the conscious mind. But the effect is still there, we still act in accordance with them and believe them to be true.

Meta Programs: These are the filters we see the world through and how we prefer to respond in certain situations, such as you may like to see things rather than feel things or the other way around.

Our meta programs are our personality types and make up our actions, behaviours and also stream into our identity.

When we understand our meta programs we understand why we do certain things, for example if you are more introvert or extrovert or perhaps even ambivert which is in the middle and can sway depending on the situation.

These really help us to understand ourselves better and help us to understand ourselves and why we act in certain ways.

Values: Our values are like an evaluation filter. They are how we decide whether our actions are good or bad, right or wrong and how we feel about our actions. Values are arranged in a hierarchy with the most important one typically being at the top and lesser ones below that. Each of us has a different set of values and our values are part of what makes up our model of the world.

When we communicate with ourselves or someone else, if our model of the world conflicts with our values or someone else's values, then there is going to be a conflict.

Our values also can change, when we experience significant emotional events in life (SEE) things like having children, changing jobs, losing someone close, moving house, experiencing a pandemic etc. We may find that the things that are important to us change and we may have what some may say 'a bit of a wake up call' I know I certainly did when I had my first child. Values are basically a deep, unconscious belief system about what's important to you individually and they help you to make choices.

When someone feels unhappy or unsatisfied in life it is usually down to the values not being met. We saw a huge world wide shift in values when we experienced the pandemic and lockdowns.

People had either found that their values were not being met or that they had changed and we saw so many people leaving jobs, starting businesses, changing careers and making big life choices and changes because everyone had gone through a SEE (significant emotional event) at the same time.

Beliefs: Beliefs are the things that we believe to be true and it's important to point out here that they are not always true. For example, blue is blue. This is true, it's a fact. We know that, everyone does. However, another belief may be "I am not good at math". Well this may not actually be true, it may just be a story someone is telling themselves and because of that then it is true as they are no longer trying to be good at maths. This is a limiting belief.

We act in accordance with our beliefs, these can be empowering, disempowering (limiting) and neutral.

For example, I love the sunshine is an empowering belief. It is hard to make money is a limiting belief that is not true and is limiting you from achieving your goals and success. Within NLP we can work on the disempowering beliefs and change the internal perceptions that you are currently running which are holding you back. When you change the way you think about things, the things you think about change.

Most of the time when people come to see me about achieving a goal, the reason they have not yet achieved it is because of a limiting belief they have about why they cannot do it. We are not always aware of these, but we always act in accordance with them anyway.

Beliefs are so deep rooted and like my example earlier, can linger from a very young age. Most beliefs we have are passed to us from our parents and we are not really sure why we have them or where they have come from. It's only when we begin to explore and become curious about what we are thinking and why that we can start to unpick these beliefs and change them.

Attitudes: Our attitudes are the way we think about things. Whether we think of the glass as being half full or half empty. How we approach things in life and the attitude that we have towards life in general.

126 BPS: This is the amount of information our minds can process at a time. Out of the millions of potential information it is broken down by the NLP model of communication process and our RAS (reticular activating system) determines what we are going to have on our internal perception.

State: This is the way that we feel. How we think determines how we feel. This can change based on how we filter the information in and what we are thinking about at the time. We can change the way we feel at any time by changing the internal perceptions we have. We can also change the way that we feel by moving (our physiology), these things are all interlinked and changing either your internal representation, state or physiology will change the other.

Physiology: Our physiology is how we move and the way we hold ourselves. Based on the internal representations we have and the way we feel will affect our physiology. If you are feeling unhappy for example you may find yourself with your shoulders slumped and chin down. However if you are feeling happy you may find yourself with your chest high, shoulders open, chin up with a kind of gleam in your face.

When we have filtered information into our internal tv (our internal representation on the left of the NLP communication model) this is linked to our state (the way that we feel) and our physiology (the way that we move). We code this in our minds in pictures to begin with and these are made up of images (visual) sounds (auditory) feelings (kinaesthetic) smells (olfactory) tastes (gustatory) and self talk (auditory digital).

Sometimes we are not consciously aware of the internal representations that we hold, however our subconscious is always aware of them and we always act in accordance with them even if you are not aware of it.

We then project this out into the world and this leads to our behaviour. The way we act, the things we do in life etc. This is why, if you have a limiting belief for example, 'he doesn't love me because I am not lovable', we can then sabotage our projection of behaviour by causing arguments or something along these lines. This is also a real life example unfortunately from some of my students and myself!

When we have empowering beliefs we then project out this behaviour, for example, 'I can do this because I am good enough', then the behaviour will mirror this and you will get a positive result. Even if you do not get a positive result straight away you will be less likely to perceive this as a failure as you will believe that it will work out if you keep trying.

Have you ever been thinking about something that has been stressing you out at the same time as trying to have a conversation with someone or sort something out and then just got really pissed off or snapped at them by mistake?

Every time I ask this question everyone raises their hand. This is because we are human and it happens to all of us. When this happens it is because of the internal representation that we have going on in our mind at that time, so when we project out our behaviour this is what comes out.

This is very normal, it doesn't feel good when it happens but now you know why it happens. It is because in our minds we are distracted with something else and we are not being present in the moment with what is in front of us.

It's hard to let things go and depending on your attitudes and what the situation is that is stressful it will also depend on how you may be able to cope with it fully. Sometimes we have to just allow ourselves to process our emotions or talk it out. It is important to be kind to yourself and rather than being negative towards yourself for screwing up or snapping, you can ask yourself better questions instead and we will come to this soon!

Think now about a time when you felt really relaxed, maybe you were on holiday, on a beach somewhere or in the spa. Think about that time now and imagine yourself there again.

What are the feelings you have? Relaxed?

Now take that internal representation in your mind and move it into the corner and make it really dark. Make it really dark and grey. Did you notice that the feelings went with it too?

Now bring it back, bring it back up again and make it really bright and compelling.

When we change the way we internalise information we also change the way we feel. We change our state and our physiology.

You can change the way you feel at any time, you just need to be aware of what your internal representations are. It's also important to note here that sometimes we do need to process emotions and allow ourselves to be human. This certainly is not about trying to stop any feelings or brush over anything. It's about being resourceful and supporting yourself when you are ready to change the way you feel.

Perhaps you are about to go into an important meeting or have an important conversation with someone. Maybe your kids are pulling at your strings and you need to chill. In times when you need to change your state you can do so just simply by changing your internal representations.

When working with NLP coaches you reprogram the thoughts that you have using further parts of NLP and change the neural networks in the brain to change your perceptions and projections. You are working with everything within the NLP model of communication.

Chapter 3: The Reticular Activating System

Your Reticular Activating System (RAS) is like a door in the front of your mind. When you become interested in things you begin to notice them more. For example, when you buy a new car you may notice you begin to see them everywhere.

In 2017 we went to go and buy a new car and ended up looking at a Nissan qashqai. I had never noticed one before and actually said I had never seen one before. We liked the car and bought it. All of a sudden I see the car everywhere! I am not kidding, I noticed them so much I was shocked about how many there were on the road and couldn't believe I had never noticed them before.

This happens for everything. When we set intentions. When we buy something new or when we decide we want to do something.

Our reticular activating system (RAS) picks up what we feed into it. For example, when we set goals we begin to notice opportunities we can take action upon to achieve them. Our RAS is there to 'protect us' and gives the brain information on what to take notice of and what isn't relevant.

Each second we see millions of pieces of information, David Hamilton in his book Thoughts that Count predicts we see 23 million bits of information per second! This is really where the NLP Communication model comes in, the RAS supports the brain with what information to pay attention to and what to ignore or not pay any attention to consciously. Your unconscious mind may pick up more information which it will store unconsciously.

The RAS is acting like a filter and will only let certain information through. This is why it is so important to get intentional on what you want in your life because this is then what your brain will filter through.

I remember the first time I became really intentional on what I wanted. One of the things I wrote down was to become a best selling author.

The very next day I was scrolling through my Facebook feed and my friend wrote a post about having just signed a book deal. I was so inspired by her post I sent her a message along the lines of "Wow I have just seen your post and am so inspired by your success as I just wrote down last night that I also want to become an author, congratulations".

She responded thanking me and connected me with her publisher. From that I became a best selling author for the first time and have since written books and become a multiple best selling author.

Your RAS is the science behind why manifestation works and how you manifest what you want in your life. This is why when people talk about manifesting what you want, or attracting what you want into your life they say you first have to get intentional. This is because you first have to program what you want into your RAS to then be able to notice it in your reality.

Our RAS works by filtering out the pieces of information we do not need to pay attention to and decides what we are going to pay attention to. Thinking back to the NLP Model of communication, it is estimated that we can potentially have around 11 million bits per second of information in our awareness. We couldn't possibly pay attention to that much information at once and so our RAS works sort of like a filter.

Imagine 11 million straws dropping down in front of you and you reach out and grasp some of them. You could only grab around 126 straws as that is all you can hold at one time. This is what the RAS does. You can only pay attention to 126 bits of information and so the RAS determines which information you are going to grasp.

Coming back to our model of the world and how we see our lives, our beliefs and attitudes also have a huge impact on what our RAS is picking up on and if we are not intentional enough then it can be negative and influence our lives in ways we don't want it to.

Your RAS works both ways. If you are programming negative things into your mind then you are going to see more negative things too. The media has a huge influence on this and can drastically change how people perceive information and then how they behave because of it. Think about it, if in the news, the papers, on the radio, tv and social media you are noticing a lot of talk about a certain topic then this can easily become part of your belief system because of the way you are filtering it into your RAS.

You have to be intentional on what you want filtering into your RAS because people usually do not have any idea about this, and naturally end up being fed a lot of bad news and then see more bad things in their reality because of this. Of course there are always things going on in the world that could be negative, however the way you see them and the other things you see are hugely impacted by what is coming in to your RAS.

Have you ever had an idea to do something but you haven't done anything about it because you didn't feel good enough to do it or you didn't feel capable enough? This is because your RAS has filtered that information into your reality and all your filtering is the "I am not good enough to do that" . I could write another full book just on limiting beliefs and how they impact our lives!

Back in 2013 I set up a fashion business. It was very successful. I was winning business awards, I was headhunted to go on Dragons Den and things were going amazing. My 5 year business projection was to turn over just short of a million and I was getting my business ready for a round of investment.

At the time I was also on the biggest growth accelerator program in the world through Natwest and I was working from their co-working space in Leeds. I found myself really easily being able to go and support the other businesses working from there and would often help them bring their ideas to life. However, when it came to my own business I would sit and stare at the wall and it didn't seem to matter what I did I just could not move forward and sabotaged myself and my success severely.

My RAS was pulling in "you are not good enough to do this" and that is all I could see in my version of reality. I had no idea at the time and would just tell myself that I didn't want the business and I had an internal battle with myself and my mind for about 6 months before I gave in and closed the business down.

At the time I had no idea that it was my RAS filtering the pieces of information into my mind that backed up my model of the world. It was only until after I closed the business down, later in the year I trained in NLP and began to understand all of this and why it had happened.

It is crazy how our minds can work when we are not intentional and just go about life without being aware of what is really happening in our mind.

We live in our comfort zones unconsciously. Remember a time when you got in your car to drive somewhere and you all of a sudden arrived where you wanted to go, but you have no idea how you got there?! This is because you are acting from your unconscious mind. Your mind has developed through the learning of driving how to drive and has stored this information and now understands you don't need this information consciously any longer.

What can happen in life is something will happen which will make you aware of you being sat in your comfort zone. It may even begin to feel painful sitting in your comfort zone and you know you are ready to make a change, or make a stretch into a new zone that isn't comfortable.

The problem can arise though because our neural pathways are not developed to take these new actions we can begin to feel overwhelmed, unsure and default back into the comfort zone because of fear or lack of motivation to follow through.

Commit to yourself to taking one action each day that will support you to feel outside of your comfort zone and begin to stretch you.

When you set intentions and goals of things that you want to achieve and do it creates a signal to the RAS to notice the things in your world that can back up and support you to be able to take action, like I did with the author scenario. When we are living in our comfort zones and not setting intentions we are allowing our minds to become programmed with whatever just happens to be in our world.

The news, which is usually negative and always about bad things happening in the world. The radio, which again is often based upon bad news and negative things happening in the world.

When we are becoming intentional in life we are programming our RAS and our minds to support us to see a new version of reality that we want to live in.

It is literally the building blocks of our reality.

When we are not doing anything to program our mind and we are just going about our lives we often tend to feel as though things are not working the way we want them to, or things always go bad.

If you want to change your version of reality then you must change what you are programming into your mind and you can only do this by becoming intentional and paying attention to what you want.

So many people know what they do not want. "I don't want to put on weight", "I don't want to feel sad", "I don't want to work in this job" but do you really know what you do want?

Our subconscious mind does not process negatives, so if you are saying "I don't want to put on weight" your subconscious is only picking up "put on weight".

Have you ever told yourself you are going on a diet and stopping eating the cookies like a cookie monster? What happens? All of a sudden, the cookies are the only thing you can think about and you have to have them or else! The sudden urge to have them becomes uncontrollable almost. This is because you are still fixated at the subconscious level on that thing.

However, if you were to say "I am a healthy and active person" your subconscious is processing this and will begin to act in accordance with it.

I remember back to when I quit smoking. It was the hardest thing ever because I was telling myself at the time "I am going to quit smoking" all my mind was programming was "smoking" I lost count of how many times I tried to quit but eventually I was able to give up when we planned to have our children as it went against my values to smoke whilst being pregnant. It was only when something so important came into my life that I was able to let it go and program a new reality into my world.

Back in 2020 we all experienced a huge change in our lives with the pandemic. All of a sudden the world closed down and we had to pay attention to the news to know what the heck was going on, or at least attempt to know what was going on.

I am very strict with myself and my boundaries because it is important to me what I program into my mind. One of the things I am always careful of is to not watch the news, listen to the radio or pay attention to negative headlines.

Yet when 2020 happened I couldn't. I had to know what was going on, as did everyone. I had live NLP Practitioner training fully booked for months in advance and I needed to know if I had to postpone them, cancel them or what.

I was knee deep in the news. Literally. I found myself feeling exhausted. As an empath too I found it overwhelming and anxiety inducing. One morning a few weeks in I remember waking up and not wanting to get out of bed. I felt so bad. My energy was being zapped from all the negativity and all I could see in my reality was all the shock and bad news of what was going on. I am sure so many of you can resonate with this.

I also realised that I had to do something about how I was feeling. The thing is, we cannot always control what happens around us but we can certainly control how we respond to it. At that moment I decided I had to get out of the news, I had to get out of the negativity of it all and take a step back for my own mental and emotional health.

I knew I couldn't do anything about the shit storm of a situation we were all in, but I could change what I was programming into my RAS and as a result how I was responding to the situation.

Immediately I began to reprogram my mind. Firstly becoming intentional on what I did want to feel and see in my reality instead. Then by journaling, visualising what I did want to see and feel. I had to let go of the need to try and control the situation because that is impossible. I had to focus on what I did want, rather than what I didn't want.

I instantly felt better and my version of reality also changed too. There were still a lot of bad things going on in the world, but my mind was no longer fixated on them. The thing is, those things would happen whether I think about them or not.

We also have something called a conscious critical faculty. The conscious critical faculty is the internal filter we use to understand how the world works based on all we have learnt rightly or wrongly since we were born.

It is the part of us that helps us get through life by having us automatically process that water will be wet and that a tiger would be dangerous. It is another survival mechanism in the brain and has helped us as humans stay alive!

We understand the world through this filter and we accept information that goes along with our beliefs, we quickly reject or dismiss any information that opposes our view of the world.

It acts as a filter to the subconscious mind and enables us to compare old experiences in our belief system to new situations.

Everything we encounter and every situation we meet, is compared with our existing model of the world which includes all our previous limitations and awareness of things that we cannot do.

Limiting beliefs will cause the Conscious Critical Faculty to reject ideas that could actually be beneficial to us.

If somebody already believes she cannot do something, then any suggestions that she can will be disbelieved and distrusted. It doesn't matter who the suggestion comes from, it will be rejected because it doesn't fit with the model of the world.

The Critical Faculty rejects it. Even if the person may appear to try to act upon the positive suggestion, they will do it with the expectation that they will fail and it is not going to work. Their attempt will be half hearted, even if they do not realise their attempt is half hearted their behaviour that is being projected out will not be as effective as it would have been if they hadn't rejected the information due to the critical faculty.

Then when they do not achieve the positive outcome it will be the other persons fault and they will think things like "see I knew there was no point in doing this, I knew it wouldn't work out".

It's important to note too that they are not being awkward, lazy or not trying. They genuinely are trying in their model of the world, but because of the beliefs they have about themselves and the situation their behaviour and attempt is affected and sabotaged by the limiting beliefs.

This is why coaching is so effective and why coaching is never about giving advice. Coaching is really about supporting someone to come to their own conclusions and NLP coaching helps you to clear out the path and limitations along the way so that things that will support you do not bounce off the critical faculty and you do get the desired results in life.

Henry Ford summed it up beautifully when he said this: "Whether you think you can or think you can't, you're probably right."

Our mind is programmed with everything we have learnt since we were born, it's formed with our script and model of the world.

So next time someone says to you *"it's all in your head"* think about this. Think about how powerful your mind really is. You can change the way you want to feel! At the end of the day you are the only person that shapes your experiences and ultimately your life.

You also may experience something called negativity bias.

Negativity bias is the tendency for humans to pay more attention, or give more weight to negative experiences over neutral or positive experiences. We tend to focus on the negative more than the positive due to a survival brain mechanism.

Have you ever found yourself dwelling on an insult or fixating on your mistakes? Criticisms often have a greater impact than compliments and unfortunately bad news frequently draws more attention than good.

This is why the media still sell such bad news, negative stories and have shocking headlines because this is what sells. Whether we like it or not, this is how our brains are wired and it's how we decide what to pay attention to.

The reason for this is that negative events have a greater impact on our brains than positive ones. Psychologists refer to this as the negative bias (also called the negativity bias), and it can have a powerful effect on your behaviour, the decisions you make, and your relationships. It's also why bad first impressions can be so difficult to overcome and why people make bad impressions in the first place.

As humans, we tend to:
- Remember traumatic experiences better than positive ones
- Recall insults better than positive praise
- React more strongly to negative things in our reality
- Think about negative things more frequently than positive ones
- Respond stronger to negative events than to positive ones

You could be having an amazing day and then something happens. Something that throws you off or makes you feel a bit rubbish. Then that is the only thing you can focus on and all of a sudden your whole day is ruined.

When you see your partner later that day and they ask how your day has been you reply saying it has been rubbish and you are feeling a bit crappy. This is all you can focus on and it consumes you.

This is the negativity bias at play and it's the natural way our brains are wired. Millions of years ago when we were about to be eaten by a saber tooth tiger and we had to be on high alert to ensure we didn't get made into dinner it was important for the negative bias to be in play. It kept us alive.

These days it tends to cause anxiety for no apparent reason because of the way we think. The problem is that most people do not understand how this works and when the anxious feelings come up they think that something is wrong.

Anxiety is a call to action from the subconscious mind that you perhaps need to do something, or something needs to be brought to your attention consciously. Not many people day to day are aware of this unfortunately and they think that something is wrong with them.

Nothing is wrong with you, you are just a human being, feeling human things.

Studies have also shown that negative news is also more likely to be perceived as truthful and because negative news draws more attention it's why it is still on the newsagents shelves and why celeb gossip magazines are still so popular.

When it was a life and death situation it was important to have the negativity bias in play, and there may still be some situations now where it is useful in life. However most of the time the things that it is causing is around social media, noticing no one is engaging on your posts or commenting on your photos and this is causing the negative feelings. Shock horror! This is where it is becoming a problem. This is where we need to consider what feelings are coming up and if it is just the primal part of our brains that is responding.

Negativity bias starts to play it's part in infancy. There have been so many studies done with young people to understand it.

In studies conducted by psychologist John Cacioppo, participants were shown pictures of either positive, negative, or neutral images. They then observed electrical activity in the brain. It was found that negative images produced a much stronger response in the cerebral cortex than positive or neutral ones.

Due to this surge in activity in a critical information processing area of the brain, it was found that our behaviours and attitudes are shaped more strongly by bad news, bad experiences, and negative information.

Although we no longer need to be watching that we are not going to be eaten by a saber tooth tiger in order to survive, the negativity bias is still a part of our brain and our programming so it is important to be aware of this and understand why you may feel a certain way.

Every single day it is having an impact on what you do, what choices you make, how you perceive things in your life, how you see your life and how you see yourself and other people.

This can affect your life in so many different ways. How you handle your relationships. You may be more likely to see the bad in others. When you meet new people, it can be harder to trust new people. You may find that you take negative impressions of people more than good ones and you could be paying more attention to bad news than good.

It's quite possible that you are negatively judging yourself too. I know I certainly was before I trained in NLP. I always thought the worse of myself and of every situation. I negatively judged myself and held ridiculous expectations of myself and then when I didn't meet them I would beat myself up about it. The expectations I had were never going to be met anyway, I have no idea where they even came from! When I learnt NLP, one of the biggest things I took away was that I have to release the need to try and meet any expectation and just have none. It left me feeling so much lighter, free and expansive.

Negativity bias can have an impact on your mental and emotional health and can cause you to dwell on the negatives. Negative information in your world, negative news, negative thoughts and so on. It can make it hard to be optimistic and sometimes you may think you are optimistic but deep down the negativity bias is still in play. Having the awareness of this is key, it's the first step to being able to understand yourself and your humanness.

Chapter 4: Reframing

Ask yourself a better question

Most people go about life not really questioning why they feel the way they do on a day to day basis. Just keeping on going and thinking they cannot change the way they feel or anything about how they act. They say things like "that's just the way it is", "That's just the way it has always been" and just keep on going on.

What happens if you are not satisfied with where you are at the moment though? What happens if you are feeling as though you want something to change but you feel stuck in this way of thinking and feeling?

When we become curious about the way we are thinking and feeling this changes our internal perceptions. By asking yourself better questions this changes the way that you feel. Remember back to the model of communication where we spoke about your internal images and representations. We can change these by changing the questions we ask ourselves or by changing the statements we are currently saying to ourselves into questions.

We can ask ourselves better questions which will help change our state (the way we feel) and then our physiology (the way we move) changes which makes our behaviour and our actions change.

If something is not going to plan, instead of feeling stuck in the problem, you can ask yourself a better question. This creates a state of curiosity which can completely change the outcome you are getting and stop you from feeling stuck. It opens you up to find new possibilities and allows you to gain more insight into yourself and the situations you may find yourself in.

Let me give you an example. I used to wake up in the morning and feel a bit shitty. I would look at myself in the mirror and say "Becky, you look like shit" and then I would feel even worse.

Not a great start to the day right? Every day used to start like this for me and then the day would just continue on like that. I had very negative thoughts, very negative self talk and would then also beat myself up about the way I thought and felt. This just led me down a negative loop and some days it would spiral out of control leaving me feeling as though I was going to have a panic attack.

The reason why I thought and felt like this was because I would program into my RAS bad news, negative gossip from Celeb magazines, I would watch things on tv that were very sad, negative and violent and then all I would see in my version of reality was more of this bad news and negativity which I would then (think back to the model of communication) also project out onto other people so I also thought other people thought badly of me. It also streamed into my behaviours. I felt exhausted all of the time and I remember thinking that I was tired with life. I was 22 and I was tired with life?! It is crazy to think that someone at 22 can think and feel like that, things like this happen to us all because this is how our brains are wired to work.

Most people go about life not knowing this and then end up on antidepressants for the rest of their lives. Please do not misunderstand me, there is certainly a time and place for medication and I will never recommend anyone stops taking it if they are on it. I am not a medical professional or a doctor and this is something that should not be taken lightly. However, I do believe that in some cases that by having an understanding of the mind and how your RAS works changes can be made to support your mental and emotional health before any other intervention is required.

Let's get back to what we can do about this and how we can become curious.

When I woke up in the morning the first things I would say would be statements "you look like shit Becky" so instead of saying these things to myself I would open myself up to curiously and ask myself a better question.

"I feel a bit low on energy this morning, this is interesting. What's going on here?' And then I will think about what I have been watching on tv, what I have been doing in general and what I have been programming into my RAS. I don't automatically go into overdrive to think about these things, I just ask myself the question and allow myself to ponder it.

Often in life things happen that we have no control over and can leave us feeling rubbish. Some things we can change and some things we cannot change. Sometimes we can feel stuck in a situation where we have no control over what is happening and it can leave us feeling really frustrated and as though there is nothing we can do.

We cannot change the things that happen after they have happened but we can change the way we act ,think about them and respond to them. We can ask ourselves better questions which will open up our mind to allow us to change our perspective.

The kind of questions we can ask ourselves are:

'What can I learn from this?'

This question is a great one because it allows us to think in a different way when it comes to challenges. I know I have had a lot of situations where I have felt so annoyed and stuck and then I have realized that perhaps there is something I need to learn from this experience so it doesn't happen again or so that it leads me in a different direction in life.

Sometimes we can find ourselves going through the same sorts of experiences over and over and over again and it can be very frustrating. I can recall numerous failed relationships that left me feeling as though I didn't ever want to go through that again. I had to learn something from the awful abusive situation I found myself in to then be able to move forward in my next relationship without this happening again. I had to ask myself better questions and when I did I got better answers.

'How can I improve the situation?'

Sometimes we cannot improve the situation. I certainly do not want to sugar coat anything. Sometimes in life things happen and there isn't a solution or anything we can do to improve it. We may experience a loss or something that we have to mourn over. This is human. This is expected, this is normal.

What I am referring to here is something that we may be dwelling over and we are ready to move on and change our perspective. It could be anything. This is very much tied to learning from the experience so that perhaps you do not keep reliving it in the future and you can move through it much easier if something like this again was to crop up.

It could be something as simple as waking up in the morning and feeling rubbish, or it could be something which is more significant in your life that you are ready to move through.

'What result do I want?'

Often when we get stuck it is because we do not know what we actually want. There is no intention. There is always an intention. Like the waking up in the morning example, the intention is to feel ok, or feel good and be ok with being human and having emotions to feel!

Most people go about life and just keep on keeping on. They do not think about what they want. Most people know what they do not want, but do not consider what they do actually want. When we ask ourselves this question it gives so much insight into the outcome and creates a pull from the subconscious to move towards it.

I now know if I wake up in the morning feeling a bit negative and I become curious I think about what I watched on tv the night before and what I programmed into my RAS and more often than not my internal representation is just negative due to what I had been watching the night before.

You can use this at any time of the day. It may be handy for you when you have just woke up in the morning or it may be that you have reacted in a certain way to something and you want to change the way you are thinking and feeling.

Asking yourself a better question is a very quick way to support yourself to become resourceful in any situation. Remember that sometimes the answer could be that you just want to allow yourself to feel the way you are feeling and move through an experience. However, if you ever find yourself dwelling on something, and ready to move on then asking yourself a better question will help you with this.

Chapter 5: Toxic Positivity

After the birth of my first child in 2015 I found myself becoming so lost and unsure about myself and my place in the world. I found myself creating this perception in my mind of what a mother and wife should be, do and how I should act and take care of my family.

I created this very high expectation of myself and if I'm being really honest, I wasn't really sure where that had come from or why I expected so much of myself.

At first I found myself in this warped version of trying to keep up to everything and these expectations I had set for myself. Giving my baby what she needed and keeping her happy, keeping the home clean and at the same time I had gone full drive into work mode and was driving my business forward. At the time I owned a fashion business and was doing incredibly well from the outside looking in.

I kept telling myself that everything would be ok and that I could make it all work. The biggest thing I think I lacked, was the ability to ask for help, and the ability to realise that I was not well at all.

Looking back now I see that I was lost and lonely and couldn't find the words to speak up about how I really felt and ask for help. I was brushing over my real feelings because I thought it would make me seem weak and unable to care for my baby.

It wasn't until I trained in Neuro-linguistic programming, after a year of this happening that I was able to break free from the internal judgements I held towards myself and recognise what is called toxic positivity.

When you act emotionless or brush over the things that you are feeling when you are really struggling is known as toxic positivity. It can come up in situations when things are going wrong and you are not paying attention to the actual reality of where you are and how you feel.

It's the tendency to brush over your negative feelings with positive thinking or positive affirmations. The problem is though, is that this can then leave us feeling even more guilty when we do feel these negative emotions, or when we feel down or sad in situations. We are not always able to just think on the bright side because real situations are happening that need acknowledging and as humans we need to feel them.

We have become accustomed in society to toxic positivity without even realising it.

Like in the situation I was in back in 2015. I sometimes find myself falling into this way of thinking by mistake now when having conversations with my children and if they get upset about something. I have to constantly remind myself that we need to, and we must honour the way they are feeling and teach them that it is ok to feel sad when you feel sad, it is ok to be disappointed when you feel disappointed about something. It's also important to acknowledge that as a parent, I may not understand why my child is upset about something, but for them it is very real and important to acknowledge that.

Often we find ourselves in situations where someone is telling us about something negative that has happened. We automatically revert to the 'oh it will be ok, think on the bright side' without consideration that the other person needs to feel these negative emotions to then move through them. This is especially harmful when we do it with children because it teaches them that we shouldn't acknowledge the way we feel in situations, even when it is completely normal to feel disappointed, angry or upset. It is important to honour our feelings and emotions and then we can move through them and learn from them rather than brush over them and just hope for the best.

Toxic positivity is something we really need to think about and be careful of. Often people do not realise that they are being toxic.

This is where people will try to brush over feelings and not acknowledge what is actually going on.

An example of this is where someone might be feeling a bit low and someone says how are you? And you reply telling them you are feeling a bit shit and they say "oh it will all be ok."

So many of us have grown up with this and have been told not to cry or not to be sad and this is an example of toxic positivity.

It's important to remember that the person isn't saying these things to be toxic, they are genuinely trying to help. However it is not helpful because it is brushing over emotions and making people feel as though they cannot speak about the way they feel which is unhealthy.

We need to express our emotions and allow ourselves to feel because we are human and it is very normal to feel the way we do.

When we brush over them we can make them worse and emotions can linger for time and become more eruptive.

Have you ever tried to dismiss something that is going on in your life, perhaps a partner has been annoying you and you haven't said anything and then after a while all of a sudden out of nowhere you feel like you have had enough?

This is because you have tried to brush over something for so long and it stacks like bricks, it then gets to the point where it is too high and topples over.

It is so important to acknowledge the way that you feel when you feel it to firstly avoid this happening but also because it is very normal to feel the way you do.

It happens a lot with parents and children too. I have to really be careful what I say to my children when they are upset because sometimes it just comes out "don't be sad" and this is toxic. This way of behaving has become so ingrained in us that we don't even know we are doing it.

Instead of saying to children "don't cry" we can talk to them about how they are feeling and thinking and what they are experiencing to allow them to move through it and process it properly when they are ready.

It helps with development and it helps children to become more emotionally intelligent.

Think about what you are saying to yourself too. If you are trying to brush over the way you feel and not properly exploring the way you are thinking and feeling you may be suppressing emotions.

It is important to allow yourself to move through your emotions because otherwise they can also become trapped energy and become toxic for the body too.

Remember back to the NLP model of communication, part of our model of the world is energy, time and space. This is so important because you do not want to trap any negative energy inside, you want to allow yourself to process it thoroughly and move through it.

So, when it comes to it, where does neuro-linguistic programming fit into all of this?

Neuro-linguistic programming is a powerful mindset and set of methods you can use to help yourself and your thinking. It is certainly not about brushing over the way you feel but about acknowledging what is happening in the moment and then helping yourself if for example you find yourself like I did, placing too much of an expectation on yourself that you are never able to live up to. Or if you find yourself dwelling on a situation for too long and it is affecting your life and every day.

A very simple way you can use NLP to help yourself in situations where you have acknowledged the way you feel and need help to move through it is to ask yourself a better question.

Using NLP can help in all areas of life. When it comes to the way we think and the way we attach meaning to things the best method within NLP is to ask better questions. It's very simple really, yet a very powerful way to reframe your thoughts and the way you attach meaning to things.

Just by asking yourself a better question you can change the way you think in a moment and become more resourceful. Depending on what situation you are in may depend on the question, however a universal question that will help you change the way you think would be "What can I learn from this situation that is personal, positive and about the future?"

By asking yourself this question you are opening up your mind to think of how this current reality will support you in the future, and if you are unsatisfied with the current situation you will begin to think of positive resources and how this will support you into the future.

When I teach NLP to my students we talk a lot about how we perceive reality in the first place. This is part of what caused me to create this unrealistic expectation of myself and then never be able to live up to it. It is important to understand how we perceive our reality and how we filter events into our minds. Our brains are wired to notice all the things that back up what we currently believe in our reality. Everyone has a different version of reality and everyone has different beliefs, values, personalities and attitudes. This is what determines what we filter into our reality.

When we believe that something bad is going to happen, or we think negatively or emotionally about a situation the part of our brain called the Reticular Activating System is designed to then notice anything you experience going on around you in this way.

You will only filter through the things that back up what you already believe and what you are already thinking. We first need to become aware of this. When we understand that the way we think and feel in the moment will only attract more of the same stuff then we can do something about it and we can begin to ask ourselves better questions.

When it comes down to it, it is important to recognise the way you feel in the moment. Allow yourself to honour that feeling and feel into it. Be curious and then allow yourself to move through it. If you need some extra support to move through the emotions as and when the time is right, then you can ask yourself a better question. "What can I learn from this situation?

If you find yourself still trying to brush over negative experiences and emotions then journaling can really help you to get everything going on in your head out and onto paper.

Just by starting simply by writing down what you can see in your surroundings, then moving into what you can hear and then finally what you are feeling. This will really help you to acknowledge what is happening in the moment and instead of brushing over it and not honouring your humanness, you can appreciate yourself and your experiences in the good times and the bad.

Remember:

- What you put in to your mind you will project out
- If you spend all of your time watching soaps and TV then you are going to be walking around with corrie goggles on
- When we feed our mind and soul with learning and development we grow as individuals personally and professionally

- Be aware of what you are doing with your time
- Feed yourself well
- Drink plenty of water
- Nourish your body and your mind
- Think about how you are starting your day and what you are doing in your morning routine

It's easy to blame other people for when things don't go to plan. When something goes right we are usually really happy to take responsibility but when it comes to things going wrong people usually blame other people.

When we take responsibility for the things that happen in our lives we are in control of our outcomes. We cannot control things outside of ourselves and other people but what we can control is the way we react and the way that we act.

Would you like to be in the driving seat and are you responsible for your own life? Ask yourself better questions as we have already discussed and focus on your end results and your goals.

We can start taking action and know what action we need to take in order to get the results we want in our lives.

Earl Nightingale said The mind is like land, whatever you plant it will grow, regardless.

Whatever you plant in your mind, you will get out. If you plant dandelions you will get dandelions, if you plant roses you will get roses.

Think of it like a sausage machine, you have to put sausage in to get sausage. Understanding our model of the world and feeding ourselves with goodness, learning and development we will get out what we want.

Understand yourself, how do you want to feel everyday, and what do you need to nourish yourself with in order to feel that way?

William James - the author of The Principles of Psychology and known as the grandfather of psychology introduced cause and effect back in the 1900s. William devoted much of his life to the research and was a big player in bringing the science of mental health closer to the mainstream.

He wanted to know, how much of our life is created by ourselves and how much is determined outside of ourselves? Do we have any control over our lives and the quality of our lives?

He couldn't put a % on the outcome but what he did find is that those people who felt as though they had no control over their lives and blamed everything other than themselves were unhealthier, unhappier and didn't feel fulfilled in their lives or jobs.

People who are more positive and take personal responsibility for their outcomes are proven to be more happier, healthier and get better results in their lives.

Bob Proctor the author of Thoughts are things said "Thoughts become things. If you see it in your mind, you will hold it in your hand."

If we think "failure", then failure will be transmuted into reality. If we think of success", then success will be transmuted into reality.

It is always much easier to focus on the negative than the positive, but when you switch your mind around you will achieve much greater results and feel much happier in life.

It is also important to note that sometimes you can be at cause for one thing in your life and then for something else you may be at effect. At the same time.

An example of this is something that happened in my own life.

Years ago when I was toilet training my youngest child. We decided at the same time to get a puppy, not taking into consideration that we needed to potty train them both at the same time.

While this was all going on I had a big marketing campaign running in my business that I had full control over and it was going really well. I had taken full responsibility for this and had even let go of a limiting belief I had previously held around it of not having enough time to make it work. I was fully at cause for this and knew that if I just took personal responsibility then I would get the result I wanted.

Now, back to the toilet training. My sister had sent me a message asking me how I was and I began writing a longgggggg story to her about why it was so difficult to toilet train my little girl, whilst having a puppy and doing everything else I needed to do.

As I was writing it I realized that I was being at effect. I was moaning about why I couldn't do what I needed to do, why everything was so hard and why it was impossible.

As I read it back to myself I decided to delete it, and just get on with it. I realized I needed to take personal responsibility and just get the result that I wanted. Within two weeks both my little girl and the dog were toilet trained!

When we take personal responsibility for the things in our lives we are able to get much better results and take action easier. It propels us forward to get the end result and even if things don't work out straight away we will still move towards the things we want much easier.

Cause: People who understand that they are in control of their lives and they can change their results if they choose. They achieve what they desire in life and they know they have a responsibility to change their actions if they want to change their results.

Effect: Blame everything and everyone other than themselves for their problems. They have lots of reasons and excuses as to why they are not living the life they want. Most people are not aware of being in the effect, good indications to look out for in yourself and others is the language you are using, the words you use. The reasons and excuses you are using as to why you are not getting the results you want in your life.

You cannot be in the cause and effect at the same time. When in the effect box you are giving away your personal power, and you are not taking responsibility. You cannot change what others do but you can change the way you respond.

When you are not in a great state, you are usually in the effect box. You can bring yourself back into the cause box by asking yourself within one specific situation, but you can be in cause for one thing in your life and effect for a different thing in your life.

In Think and Grow Rich written by Napoleon Hill in 1937 and has sold over 15 million copies, he talks about surrounding yourself by people who you aspire to be like, with mentors and people you look up to. I like this principle, because the kind of people you want to be surrounding yourself with will be in the cause box, they will have personal responsibility of their lives and they will be in control of their outcomes.

Personal responsibility is like the corner stone of NLP, when releasing the victim attitude you will feel much lighter, and you will begin to get much better results in your life. Sometimes it may slip, not all of us are perfect, we have to practice, just like we rehearse a stage show. We rehearse and rehearse for months ahead of time before going out centre stage, and even then it's not perfect. That's ok, remember this is your life and you are in control of the way you act, and the way you respond to the events in your life.

Chapter 6: Beliefs

A while ago I was researching getting an extension built on my home. I was ringing around getting quotes and speaking to people about who to use. I had a conversation with my brother about it and mentioned I was getting Coral windows out to quote. At the time I thought it was going to be a conservatory rather than a full extension.

He said not to speak to Coral because they are rubbish. Before I learnt about NLP I would have just taken what he said straight away and not questioned it, however something made me question why he had this belief and so I asked "What makes you think that" and he replied "Oh, I don't know actually".

Sometimes we form beliefs and we don't even know where they have come from. We then accidentally project these beliefs on to other people without realising it and they may then become that person's belief too.

Sometimes this can work to our advantage, for example if our children are playing somewhere dangerous and we want them to stop so we tell them to. Beliefs are thoughts that we have about something that we believe to be true. We can have empowering beliefs and also limiting beliefs. Sometimes we will just take on what someone has said and believe it straight away, especially if we trust that person.

They are formed by the events that happen in life, once you have a few stocked up in your memories you create a belief that you believe to be true in your model of the world. We usually take on beliefs around the imprint period between ages 0-7.

Within the ages of 0-7 we are like sponges, soaking up everything that is going on around us and creating our perception of the world and our place in it. We begin to understand how things work in different ways, what outcomes we get with certain behaviours and we take in everything going on around us.

Beliefs can be formed from observing and listening to our teachers, our parents and the people we are surrounded with between the ages of 0-7. Beliefs are formed throughout the whole of our lives, every day we are making choices, creating new beliefs or perhaps changing the beliefs we have. Our deep rooted beliefs mostly but come from the imprint period.

We carry around our beliefs within our model of the world for the rest of our lives, often never questioning why we have them or where they came from. Often my students will discover their limiting beliefs through training and they cannot believe they have been carrying things through their lives for so long. I recall one student in her 50's telling me that she had been carrying around limiting beliefs from the age of 7 her whole life. This was impacting her life, the choices she made and everything she did. Due to something that is completely irrelevant to her life now.

This is how beliefs work. They are deeply rooted in the subconscious mind and they can be sneaky.

A limiting belief or a limiting decision is something that we say to ourselves and possibly others that stops us from achieving something in our lives. This can be a goal, or it can be just day to day life and it affects the quality of our lives. It can stop us from thinking things are possible for ourselves and really limit our potential, in manifesting and attracting the things that we want in our lives. We can have limiting beliefs in all areas of our lives, our personal lives, business, career, family and relationships.

At 24 I ran a successful fashion business. I was winning business awards, I was on the biggest growth accelerator in the world, I was invited to go on to Dragons Den and pitch my business, we were getting investment ready to run a round of funding and we had people interested. I would see people in the local shop from school and they would say "Wow, Becky you are doing so amazing since school!" Inside it would make me cringe and I hated it.

I had an internal battle with myself about the running of the business, I would go to the office and sit staring at the wall with no idea what to do to move forward, even though I had a step by step strategy and plan of action.

During this time I had my first baby and as it came to a head she was about 6 months old. I had known I was struggling with post natal depression when I first had her, but I had no idea it was still going on 6 months later.

I was positive, I was making things work, things appeared to be going very well on the outside. However, on the inside I felt awful, I tried to brush over it (very toxic) and tried to just keep going, being the 'positive' person I am.

I didn't realise it until I had trained in NLP but I had so much negative self talk going on, and I had this warped perception of myself and who I should be. I was appalled with myself when I didn't meet up to this and I never met up to it, because I have no idea where this warped perception came from. I have no idea why I ever set this bar so high of what I expected from myself because no one, especially not a woman who had just had a baby and was running a business would be able to meet it.

I felt like I couldn't ask for help and I felt like I had nowhere to turn. Which is crazy, because there were so many people and places to get help around me. I tried to block it all out and it manifested itself in self sabotaging behaviours.

I told myself I didn't want to run my business and then another part of myself told me I did want to run the business and that I would be a huge failure if I closed it down.

This internal battle went on for what felt like forever and I felt exhausted every day. Eventually I decided to close down the fashion business and I went back to a sales job I had held before starting my business.

It felt like a huge relief and through being back at this male dominated sales job I realized that I needed some extra tools and techniques to help train my team and support my sales staff.

When I went back to this role I was told I wouldn't be managing people, but within a month I had found myself getting a promotion and managing the team again, I couldn't help myself.

The company trained its managers to lead by fear. To sack people when they didn't meet their sales targets and to only ever dangle carrots. It didn't feel right to me and something was off.

As I began to look for sales training for myself that was when I stumbled on NLP. I was listening to the Tony Robbins Unlimited Power CD on repeat and when I had set the intention to look for sales training that was when I heard Tony say NLP - Neuro-Linguistic Programming and that is when I knew I had to complete this training.

As I began the training I realised that I had closed my fashion business because I didn't believe in myself or my abilities in making the business work. It became clear to me that I had sabotaged my success even though at that time I had no idea what the word sabotage even meant, let alone how it manifested in my life.

I hadn't felt good enough to grow my business and I hadn't felt worthy of having the success that I had created. Looking back now, I realise that nothing I could have done would have made it work because I had no idea that these things were going on at the subconscious level and we ALWAYS act in accordance with our beliefs. Even when we are not aware of them.

We always act in accordance with what we believe, whether it is a negative belief, a positive belief or a neutral belief, we always act in accordance with them because these form the basis of our lives. These are what makes us feel stable, even when they are not true.

When we have limiting beliefs it impacts the way we behave, the actions we take, the results we get, what we manifest into our lives and what we attract.

Thinking back to my beliefs, when I was going through my NLP training for the first time I explored my beliefs and where they had come from.

I identified that my limiting belief that was impacting my life the most was not feeling good enough. Not feeling good enough as a mum, as a wife, as a caregiver, as a business owner, as a woman, I didn't feel good enough in any area of my life.

When I thought back to the first time I didn't feel good enough, it was when I was about 6 and I was singing the Aqua Dr Jones song out loud. I had one of those cassette players with some earphones and I loved the song.

My sister shouted at me and told me I am rubbish at singing. This was the first time I remember not feeling good enough.

The next time I remember not feeling good enough I was 6 and playing in the school playground. I want to play with some kids and they don't want to play with me. This was another chalk up for the 'I am not good enough' belief.

Throughout my life one of the constant things has been dance. I have always danced and (fun fact) I am a trained dance teacher! I remember at a young age I was asked if I wanted a solo part in the show, but then this never happened and it made me think 'perhaps I am not good enough for that'.

All of a sudden we have this tally of external events that have been deleted, distorted and generalized and filtered into the model of the world to mean 'I am not good enough'.

It is important to note, that this isn't anyone else's fault, it's not about putting blame on others. It is about being aware of the way that we have filtered in information and deleted, distorted and generalised the information we have been presented with in our external events. Think back to the NLP Model of Communication.

This is also not the truth. It is just the way that we have distorted information as we have filtered it into our model of the world and the meaning we have given to it.

My sister who told me I was rubbish at singing was also a child too. My dance classes I attended, my mum couldn't manage to pay for the lessons once a week let alone extra lessons for the solo parts.

We don't always have all of the information presented to us in our external events, and this is important to note.

Beliefs are formed by points of reference that we store in our minds to make sense of our model of the world. Some of the major ones about relationships, money, love, and how we feel about ourselves. These tend to be formed in the imprint period.

All beliefs are made up in your own model of the world and they are a construct of what you believe to be true. You can change your beliefs as you choose but you have to first be aware of what your beliefs are to then be able to change them or release them.

Roger Bannister, the middle-distance athlete and neurologist decided back in the 1950's that he would break the record for the four-minute mile run. Back then everyone believed that if you were to run that fast you would die. That your lungs would burst and you wouldn't be able to function.

Then other runners also began running the mile in less than 4 minutes. Did humans change? No, it was the belief of what is possible that changed.

Perception is projection. What we perceive in our minds we will then project out on to the others, on to the way we behave, on to the way we interact and communicate with ourselves, others and the environment.

What beliefs do you have that are limiting you?

You may not consciously be aware of the beliefs you have, they are all deeply buried in your unconsciously but we act in accordance with our beliefs because we act in the confines of what we believe to be true.

NLP is about looking through a different perspective and challenge the beliefs and things that are holding you back. Whenever you are using a reason as to why you cannot do something you need to take notice of what the internal self talk is and ask yourself what are the beliefs you have. Are they empowering you or are they limiting you?

Henry Ford said If you think you can do a thing or think you can't do a thing, you're right. This sums up perfectly what a limiting belief is. If you change your belief to believe you can, then you will.

I teach within my NLP certification courses how you release and change limiting beliefs for yourself and for your clients.

Remember your RAS (Reticular Activating System) will let in what you let in, based on your beliefs and your model of the world. Limiting beliefs also work in the same way with the RAS so if you have a limiting belief the RAS will let in and notice information to accompany the belief.

This is then distorted and generalised in your model of the world, which is your own representation of the world which is not real for everyone. We then have the self talk going on all of the time and we can change this by asking better questions.

The most effective people know they are in control of their lives and the outcomes that happen.

I touched on self sabotage earlier, so let's circle back.

Self-sabotage is when we sabotage our efforts of achieving the things that we want to achieve before achieving it or after achieving it. It might happen before we actually take any action as this in itself is a form of self sabotage or it may be that we start taking action and begin to see some results but then we stop the action and we don't really know why.

It is born from a limiting belief and usually, the limiting belief is something between the lines of I'm not good enough, I'm not worthy, I don't deserve that, and we may have no idea that these beliefs are actually there.

Although we may not be aware of them, they are still there and then we act in accordance with our beliefs. Within our minds we create internal perceptions and if we have a belief of not being good enough or a limiting belief like this then we will act in a way that creates a reality for us to match it. This is self sabotage.

We may not be consciously aware of it, but it is still happening.

Because of these beliefs we then act in certain ways to screw up the things that we have achieved or that make us happy. E.g. causing an argument with a partner, telling yourself you don't want to do something, binge eating when you are on a weight loss journey.

If you would like to understand further if you are experiencing self sabotage or discover what block you may be coming up against at the moment then check out my quiz that helps you determine your blocks and challenges. You can find it on the website www.YesICanMethod.com

How to identify a limiting belief in yourself or others?

1. You are giving reasons as to why things are not the way you want them rather than getting results.

2. You tell yourself a story about why you haven't got what you want in life, rather than taking action.

3. You are saying negative things to yourself about yourself.

4. You blame things around you that are outside of your control for not being able to do things you want.

The most common limiting beliefs that I hear are 'I am not good enough' or 'I am not worthy of ...' You may identify limiting beliefs that you are conscious of, such as 'I cannot make sales', or 'I am not good at sales' for example. Usually these are caused from a deep rooted limiting belief of I am not good enough, or I am not worthy. I always recommend working on these bigger ones if you can as they will knock out the smaller ones.

The techniques that I teach within my Neuro Linguistic Programming and Breakthrough Coaching course and my other courses to help with these are:

1. Time Line Therapy™

2. Submodalities Belief change

3. Quick belief change chat

4. Use language patterns to release and open up model of the world (Practitioner – Meta Model, Master Practitioner – Quantum Language patterns)

5. The 6 steps to unravel a belief

It is important to remember that we have to consistently work on ourselves and apply this on going. I check in with myself each week and work on limiting beliefs.

If you have identified the limiting belief in yourself, and you're consciously aware of it, the 6 steps to unravel a belief is a powerful technique to help you get rid of limiting belief:

Ask yourself the following questions:

1. What is the belief?

2. Why do I believe it?

3. What am I afraid will happen if I don't believe that?

4. Do I believe that?

5. Whose belief is that?

6. What can I believe instead that will support me?

<u>Chapter 7:</u> Rapport

Rapport is the basis of every effective communication. That feeling when communication just flows and there is an easy flow to liking someone and you have things in common. It's easy to have a conversation with someone when you are in rapport. It feels good to have rapport.

When you are in rapport with people it is easy to get along and have better relationships. It starts with you personally and it is up to us to be good at rapport, we understand that we have control of our outcomes and how we can build relationships with the people around us.

When you know how to build rapport, it is easy to build relationships with new people and make the existing relationships feel better and more solid. It's helpful for coaching, for working with clients, for teaching and also for our close ones.

Rapport is a feeling of being in-sync with someone else, to be on the same wavelength and consequently to really understand and appreciate someone else and their opinions.

7% of communication is down to the words we use.

38% of communication is the tonality, how it is being said.

55% of communication is down to physiology.

We have an impact on everyone around us even when we don't know them, a lot gets communicated through our physiology. Communication comes from so many different sources, email, phone in person.

Richard Bandler and John Grinder, the founders of NLP, modelled excellent communicators. One of the people they modelled was Dr Milton Erickson, he spent around 60 years of his life doing Hypnosis and got amazing results. He would mirror and match the physiology of his clients to build rapport. He didn't know he was doing this, his clients received amazing results and experienced clients had rapid transformations. Rapport is the basis of NLP.

We can match and mirror physiology unconsciously. When we are comfortable and at ease with the people we are around it becomes a natural thing to do. It's not always essential to completely mirror someone to build rapport, just some mirroring and matching can make a difference.

Matching & Mirroring

Imagine there is a mirror between you and the other person. You follow the physiology of the person you are with. Notice the next time you are in a cafe people sitting together, are they mirroring and matching each other's body language?

Matching could also be your client tapping a foot on the floor, whilst you tap your pen on a book using the same rhythm. This is called cross over matching and mirroring - using a different part of your physiology to match another person.

The different ways we can build rapport are through;

Physiology

Physiology: Body language and the way we move. You can mirror the way someone is sat down or stood up. You don't have to fully mirror the way they are standing as it may be unnatural or feel a bit awkward. What you could do for example, is if someone has their legs crossed, you could just cross your ankles. This is still mirroring. Facial expressions and blinking are also ways to match physiology. Blinking is a great one to use with babies and animals to build rapport and relax babies when they are feeling unsettled.

Breathing is one of the biggest indications you are in rapport with someone. Pay attention to the location of breathing. It could be high up in the diaphragm or low in the stomach and the speed of breathing, fast, medium or slow. These are all things you can match and mirror, and they come in useful when you have a client and you are building a relationship.

Tonality of our voice The words we use

Tonality: We can match and mirror someone's tone - the pitch of their voice. The tempo of someone's speech, and the timbre or quality of their voice and the volume. We have 93 tones to our voice but we only usually use 3/4 tones on a day to day basis. Try this out the next time you are speaking to someone on the phone and see how much you can build rapport.

The words we use: People use different words and have different meanings to words. Some people may use phrases often that we don't use and by using these phrases and words in a conversation it will help build rapport. Don't use them too much as this could break rapport, but using them here and there can help build the relationship.

Sharing **common experiences** will also help build rapport "Oh, where did you go on holiday?" It can be more natural to build a relationship this way and I would always lead this way.

Chunk Sizes. We all talk in different chunk sizes. Some people like talking about the big picture and bigger ideas and plans. Other people prefer to talk about the smaller details and the step by step actions and smaller things and details. By matching someone's chunk size you will keep them interested in what you have to say as someone who is big picture may appear to get bored in the detail and someone who is into the details may feel like something is being missed out when someone talks to them in higher levels of information.

Observe people around you when you are out and about and notice when people are in rapport or completely out of rapport notice the differences.

A good indication you are in rapport is when you are talking to someone and you move to take a drink for example and they also take a drink. If they don't follow you, it doesn't mean they are not in rapport, it could just mean they don't want a drink.

You know when someone is in rapport by the physiology, tone of voice and the words they are using. You can also use sensory acuity.

The aim of sensory acuity is to read what someone is thinking by reading their physiology, tone of voice, colour of skin tone rather than mind reading what people are thinking. What do you actually see in physiology, what can you see in front of you - this is using sensory acuity.

Sensory Acuity

I was working with a client on changing some things that she has not been happy with we were chatting through the options for her and I decided to use a technique called likes to dislikes that helps you to stop liking something that you like a bit too much and eat too often for example drinking too much fizzy pop and wanting to stop.

She found that she was picking up these bad habits and it was not helping her with her intention of being more healthy and losing a bit of weight and it was affecting her mindset and leaving her feeling a bit negative. It's important to note that it was her conclusion that she wanted to stop eating this certain thing and I didn't suggest it.

As we were going through the process I could tell at one point just by watching her facial expressions and her movements that she didn't want to let go of this thing. She was holding on to it tightly. Without my sensory acuity skills I may have missed this all together and we wouldn't have got the desired result from the NLP technique.

I was able to use what's called Sensory Acuity.

Sensory acuity is the ability to be able to notice what is happening in front of you when you are looking at a person. Understanding their facial expressions, their movements and noticing if there may be something not quite right.

We all use this already but just don't know it. Have you ever had a vibe about someone and perhaps you just haven't been able to put your finger on it? This is you using your sensory acuity skills. It's just that most people are not aware that this is what they are doing.

When you use your sensory acuity skills you are picking up if someone may be annoyed, upset, or perhaps you are having a conversation with someone and they are telling you everything is ok but you can see that something still doesn't appear quite right.

Using your sensory acuity skills helps you to determine how someone is thinking and feeling without assuming or mindreading.

Mind reading is where you are making things up in your head about what people may be thinking and feeling without any evidence to back it up. When you use your sensory acuity skills it enables you to actually take information from what you can see in front of you and can stop any confusion with mind reading.

When you use your sensory acuity skills you can easily read someone's expressions and body language so that you have a full understanding of what they could be thinking because you are taking in the information that is in front of you and using that information to make an evidence based opinion rather than jumping to conclusions about what you think may be happening.

Sensory acuity will support you to fully read someone's facial expressions and body language so instead of second guessing or mind reading, you will have the knowledge and the full understanding of how they are likely to be thinking.

It is a really helpful skill to have and helps you to pick up other people's vibes without judging or putting your own opinion on to things. Sensory acuity is like having a heightened awareness of what is going on with other people and being able to collect that information with evidence you can see in front of you.

Sensory acuity allows you to see the difference between facts and what you may be projecting onto others.

For example, you may look at someone with their arms folded and say they are bored. When in fact they may be cold.

Sensory acuity is the ability to be acutely aware of the detail in front of you, for example: mouth turned up or down, changes in skin tone, where the client is breathing from or changes in breathing. Making a conclusion that someone is cold rather than bored or something can make a huge difference in the way you communicate with them. The way you perceive information from others is crucial to the way you think about them and about yourself.

The things you notice when using sensory acuity could be:

- If their lips are turned up or turned down
- The skin colour eg, are they blushing
- The face may be longer and more drawn out
- Are the pupils dilated or glazed
- Are they breathing fast or slow

Skin colour - Can go from light to dark as the blood flows into the facial area, the face will go darker.

Skin Tonus - The shininess of someone's face, if someone is smiling they will reflect more light which indicated happiness. Cheek muscles narrow and is less shiny when you are feeling unhappier.

Breathing - Can move from fast to slow and can change in the area you are breathing in. From shoulders, to stomach. You may notice when people become more excited and you will notice them getting more excited and they will then breathe higher up in the diaphragm.

Lower lip size will be fuller than the upper lip. Sometimes the lower lip may be fuller so less lines or thinner so there are more lines.

This is all the information that you can see in front of you. Sensory Acuity is really useful when you learn NLP.

This is all about developing and learning how to pick up on sensory acuity unconsciously and learning how to read physiology rather than assuming what people are thinking by 'the look on their face'.

You may only see a few of these things we just talked about. The reason we are learning this is because we know we can observe physiology, and we may have now fallen into the habit of assuming what people are thinking. Sensory Acuity helps to read the other person and observe their physiology and notice the difference in people's state.

All of this is in the control of the unconscious mind, we don't consciously know we are changing our face and our breathing is changing. It is helpful to know about sensory acuity as it will help with a coaching relationship to pick up if a client is troubled or even if a friend you are supporting.

If you are picking up sensory acuity and you are unsure of what you are reading from the person you are speaking to, you can also just ask people "What are you thinking?"

The aim is to release any judgments we have made about what people are thinking and to have the facts to understand how and why people think the way they do.

Chapter 8: The Presuppositions of NLP

The presuppositions of NLP are like the mindsets of NLP. It's what we believe and agree to when we learn and precise NLP to use in our lives, in our business and for ourselves.

The presuppositions are important because they give us a guideline to ensure that we are using NLP for good and that we are using it to allow us to be more resourceful, develop more and become more self aware.

NLP contains a powerful set of tools and techniques that change the neural networks in the brain and are very powerful. You can make a great shift using NLP, you need to ensure you are using it in the right way and that you are using it ethically.

These presuppositions are the most common ones you will hear within NLP circles and can mean something different to each person. I will go through them with you and share what they mean to me and give you some examples of what they mean to help explain it a bit better.

People have all of the Resources they need to Succeed and to achieve their Desired Outcomes (There are no unresourceful people, only unresourceful states)

This statement suggests that we all have everything we need already and that we just need to be able to access it. Think back to the model of communication and how we filter external events. Based on how we filter in these events will depend on how we feel (our state) If we have limiting beliefs or negative beliefs then some things may be filtered in and leave us feeling Unresourceful. If we can change the way that we filter in information by changing our beliefs, the way that we feel and our internal representations then we can clear out anything that is keeping us from being resourceful.

Respect for the other person's Model of the World

Everyone has a different model of the world and everyone sees things differently. We all have different lives and experiences and due to this we perceive things differently. We must respect that everyone has a different version of the world, meaning everyone has different personalities, different opinions, beliefs and values. We must respect that people see and think things differently.

Everyone is doing the Best they can with the Resources they have available at that time (Behaviour is geared for adaptation, and present behaviour is the best choice available. Every behaviour is motivated by a positive intent)

Imagine you are walking up the street and you see a mum shouting at her child. You may think "oh gosh, I hope I don't shout at my kids like that" and you may unconsciously or consciously judge her, thinking that you'd never do that if it were you. Now imagine you walk up the street seconds earlier and you notice the child walks out into the street without looking as a car is coming. Now you have a very different perspective on the situation. The mother was only acting in accordance with the fear that she experienced at that moment in time and the behaviour that was available was based on trying to protect the child. It was never coming from a bad place, it was coming from a place of love, fear and protection.

Signs of Resistance in a client is a Sign of a Lack of Rapport (There are no resistant clients, only inflexible communicators. Effective communicators accept and utilise all communication presented to them)

When we do not connect with someone and build rapport it can be hard to have a conversation with them. When we do build rapport we end up in lengthy conversations and high energy. When you are in communication with anyone around you it is important to build rapport with them to help you communicate more effectively.

You are in Charge of your Mind, and therefore your Results (I am also in charge of my mind and therefore my results)

This is all about taking personal responsibility. Being aware that you are in charge of your actions and your results and no one else can do it for you. It is up to you to get the outcomes you want and you cannot put it on to someone else. So many people go through life thinking that they have no control over their lives and what happens, but if we do not have control, then how do we make changes to things that we are not happy with?

Procedures should Always be Designed to increase Wholeness Procedures should Always be Designed to increase Choice

This is about ensuring that NLP is used for good. We should always be using NLP to open up our minds and create more choice and peace in our everyday being.

Observe and Calibrate on Behaviour: The most important information about a person is their behaviour

Sometimes someone might say something but mean something else. Or someone may really think they believe something but when it comes down to it they actually are projecting out a different thing from their model of the world. An example of this is when I had my fashion business that I closed down. I really thought that I believed in myself and if you'd have told me I had a limiting belief I would have laughed. I really was not aware of it at all! Yet my behaviour showed something different. Although I told myself I could do it, I still closed the business down and went back to employment.

The System / Person with the most Flexibility of behaviour will Control the System.) - The Law of Requisite Variety

If something is not working and you are not getting the results you want you can change your approach. If that doesn't work then you can change your approach again. The law of requisite variety is really about understanding that if something isn't working we can evaluate it, and then change what we're doing and then continue this process until we get the outcome and the result that we do want.

In Communication - The Meaning of your Communication is the Response that you get

One day I was in the car with my two little girls and we were driving somewhere. My eldest said "mummy, please can we go to that place we went before" so I replied "which place Eva." "You know mummy, that place when we drove up there and went that way" as she pointed up the road. I replied "I'm not sure where you mean Eva". She began to get annoyed and raised her voice "you know mummy, that place!" She continued to repeat the same words but raised her voice and continued.

How many times have you done that? When you have been talking to someone and they haven't understood what you are meaning and you get annoyed and raise your voice, repeating the same thing you had just said.

When we are communicating with someone we need to change the words we are using if they do not understand us. This is really about taking responsibility for the way people interpret our language and our communication.

Only Feedback! - There is no failure, only feedback

There is no such thing as failure only feedback! I love this one. Sometimes when we are working towards something it doesn't go to plan and often this can stop us from moving forward. If you were to believe that there is no failure and only feedback wouldn't you continue to move forward?

Everything that comes back to us is information and what we do with that information is critical. If something isn't working we can evaluate, take the feedback and then move forward. This is very closely linked with the law of requisite variety.

Not their Behaviour - People are not their behaviours (Accept the person; change the behaviour)

One day when my eldest child first started school I had a rough night. My youngest was a baby at the time and she hadn't slept well that night. We all slept in and then was rushing around a bit to get ready in the morning for school. I put the kids shoes and coats on and ran upstairs quickly to go to the loo before leaving. When I came back down they had both removed their coats and shoes. I picked up the baby and shoes and began walking down the steps getting overwhelmed and anxious at this point because we were going to be late and my eldest then refused to put her shoes back on. I erupted and began shouting at her to put her shoes on. I threw the shoes to the floor and pleaded with her to put them on. She was devastated that I had shouted at her as I had never shouted at her like that before and she began to cry, then the baby began to cry and then I began to cry because I was shocked at my shouting that just came from nowhere.

I am not shouting. I am not anger. These are not my identity, they are behaviours that are not me, and that I rarely exhibit too. People are not their behaviours.

Chapter 9: Goal setting and NLP

I've left this section until the end because I wanted you to know everything you now know before you begin to get really down to it with goals.

I did introduce right at the start for you to get intentional on what you want from this book, so now we are going to move into goal setting using NLP and how you can tie everything you have learnt in this book together.

Thinking back to the model of communication and the RAS, setting goals and becoming intentional is the first step to being able to decide what you program into your mind and how you then respond to it.

What you see in your version of reality is based on what your intentions are and how you are setting yourself up for success.

Without this you may find yourself aimlessly moving through life without any real idea on what you want and how to get it.

Some people want a nice peaceful life, this is still an intention.

Some people want to grow a large successful business, this is an intention.

Whatever it is that you want, you first need to understand what your intentions are and then you can begin to move towards them.

When you know about your intentions and what you want and you program that into your mind you create an open loop for the subconscious. This means that your subconscious mind will be searching for everything in your reality to back up the intentions that you are setting.

When you take the actions towards getting what you want you will then see more possibility and more options to move toward this too.

Often people do not set intentions and then they find themselves in a place they never wanted to be.

A job they never wanted, a town you never expected to live in and so on. When we become intentional and really know what we want we can ensure that we end up somewhere we always want to be.

Think about it like a sat nav. When you get in your car to drive to a place you have never been before you input it into your sat nav to help direct you and give you the quickest route.

We NEED to reframe success!

So many people find themselves chasing this idea of success. Chasing this something and when it comes to it they say "what next" or "what now" and it never ends.

Sometimes people get there and realise it was never what they even wanted in the first place.

We are taught in society that success means being productive, being on all the time. Having things. This is one of the biggest ones. Having things.

Even when we create vision boards we add things that we want. Things that we think will fill us up, and all of these things are outside of ourselves. They are not us and they ultimately do not bring happiness.

However, everyone wants success because they think that this will ultimately bring happiness.

Here are a few things we need to do to ensure we are checking in with ourselves and not chasing some version of success that we really never wanted:

1. **Ask yourself - is this actually my version of success? What does success mean to me?**

We see so many people doing amazing things and we think we want what they do, so we start to move towards that. Then we get there and we are unhappy, or we realise when it is too late we never wanted it anyway.

2. Being busy all the time does not equal success.

We think that when we are busy and have lots going on that this means we are successful. Is this really what you want though? How do you actually want to spend your time? This is the question you should be asking yourself.

3. Filling yourself up with things outside of yourself will not always mean success for you.

Marketing is very clever. All marketing feeds you is the idea that you have to buy something to make you feel like you are a success. To make you happy. This is so you will buy their things. Always remember this. People all the time are making themselves broke trying to look rich to other people.

Setting goals and intentions is very much like this. We are starting with the end in mind so we know where we are heading and why.

It is important to program the RAS so that we manifest what we want in life. So many people go through life knowing what they do not want, but not being intentional about what they do want.

You must become intentional and set goals, one of the ways we can do this is through a 90 day plan.

When I first set my 90 day plan I also wrote down some longer term goals too. Things such as wanting to live in a house overlooking water, wanting to be a best selling author and more.

Within 5 months I had moved into a big apartment overlooking the canal with a spa downstairs and I was part of my first book a collaboration project with other authors that became a best seller!

We have to become international to be able to achieve the things that we want, because without the intention we cannot see the possibilities or the opportunities that we can take action on to achieve our goals and dreams.

So, how do you write a 90 day plan?

Take a piece of paper, split it down the middle.

One side write 'Goals' and the other write 'Actions'.
Write a list down the Goals side of all the things you want
to achieve in the next 90 days, then on the other side
break them down into actions.

So for example, if one of my goals is 'to live in a house
overlooking water' then an action may be 'start looking on
right move for houses that may be suitable'

Action is important.

Break down each of your goals into actions and ensure
you begin to take these actions daily, you can check in with
your 90 day plan daily. Put it somewhere you will see it
often.

One of the things I go through in my other book The
Females Handbook: Step into your Personal Potential is
your 90 day plan and how to break down daily actions,
weekly actions and monthly actions to support you to
achieve the things you want much quicker. I highly
recommend you check out that book, you can find it on

Amazon if you search Rebecca Lockwood it should come up.

Action = Response from the universe.

When you move the energy around you has to move too, the universe has to respond.

Once you are intentional on what you want then check in with yourself consistently and clear out any limiting beliefs.

- Ask yourself "what do I believe about having this" and work on the limiting beliefs as they come up

- Journal as if you already have your goal

- Visualise as if you already have your goal

- Write down action steps you can take that day to achieve your goal and take action

I used to be a chaser, someone who would always once achieving something say "ok, what's next?' I would never allow myself to fully embrace the moment of actually having made it happen.

Are you allowing yourself to fully embrace your moments? Are you allowing yourself to fully enjoy the journey towards making things happen and even more importantly, are you allowing yourself to feel satisfied before you have even made anything happen?

Don't be a chaser like I used to be, it sets you up from the get go to fail. Really the ultimate goal should be to feel content with yourself, with wherever you are right in the moment, even when those moments may be challenging.

Are you facing any blocks or challenges at the moment? Is there something you are working on and you're finding yourself questioning it all the time? Find out where you may be experiencing blocks in your life right now with our deep dive quiz that will help you determine what challenges you may be experiencing right now! You can find the quiz on my training website www.YesICanMethod.com

I cannot believe we are at the end of the book. There are so many more things I would love to share with you. So many more things I would love to educate you on and so much more within NLP that you need to know! I just couldn't fit it all into one book! I would love to welcome you on my NLP courses.

You can make a start on my NLP courses for free, move and progress into my certification programs and learn how to help yourself change your mind which will change your life and then how to help others do the same if you feel called to do so.

My courses not only support you in your own life, but also equip you with the tools necessary to help others too. If you are feeling called to taking the next steps head to my website www.YesICanMethod.com and find everything we have to support you.

I always love a good share and tag on social media, so do go ahead and let me know you have read the book! A good selfie with the book is always appreciated!

You can find me and tag me on Instagram at @Rebecca.Lockwood and @the_yes_i_can_method_academy

See you there!
Lots of love, Becky x

Printed in Great Britain
by Amazon

87843584R00081